Plugged In

from boys to MEN

All About Adolescence and You

MICHAEL GURIAN

Illustrated by Brian Floca

PSS!
PRICE STERN SLOAN

Special thanks to John Garwood, M.D., Pediatrician, Mt. Sinai Hospital, New York, NY.

Library of Congress Cataloging-in-Publication Data

Gurian, Michael.
  From boys to men : all about adolescence and you / by Michael Gurian ; illustrated
by Brian Floca.
    p. cm. — (Plugged in)
  Summary: Answers questions about the physical, emotional, sexual, and social
changes that teenage boys undergo during adolescence.
    1. Teenage boys—Juvenile literature. 2. Adolescence—Juvenile literature.
  3. Puberty—Juvenile literature. 4. Sex instruction for boys—Juvenile literature.
  5. Interpersonal relations in adolescence—Juvenile literature. [1. Teenage boys.
  2. Puberty. 3. Sex instruction for boys.] I. Floca, Brian, ill. II. Title. III. Series.
HQ797.G86   1999
305.235—dc21   98-37025
                                                                        CIP
                                                                        AC

ISBN 0-8431-7483-8 (pb) A B C D E F G H I J
ISBN 0-8431-7474-9 (GB) A B C D E F G H I J

Plugged in ™ is a trademark of Price Stern Sloan, Inc.
PSS!® is a registered trademark of Price Stern Sloan, Inc.

For the boys
—M.G.

Acknowledgements
I wish to gratefully acknowledge Jane O'Connor, Emily
Neye, Katrina Weidknecht, the staff of *Price Stern Sloan*,
Susan Schulman, my wife Gail, my children, and all those
young people who have made this book possible.

table of contents

introduction

Josh is the son of a good friend of mine, and I've been close to him for a long time. He's older now, but when he was fourteen we went to see the movie *Spawn.* You may have seen it. A man gets killed but comes back to life. Suddenly he's able to grow armor, but he doesn't really understand what this armor is for. By the end of the movie, he's finally figured out what he's supposed to do with his "new life": Fight the bad guys.

Spawn is sometimes funny and sometimes sad. Josh really liked the movie, and he and I talked about it afterward. He told me that often, growing up felt like that—you don't really understand what's happening, you have to grow armor, and you have to work hard to figure out what's happening inside you and discover who you really are.

Going to the movie and listening to Josh reminded me of how confused I felt during my own boyhood. The movie about a man dying and being reborn reminded me how all over the world, in all kinds of cultures, people think of adolescence as a time when a boy dies and is reborn. The boy doesn't actually die, but boyhood dies and manhood is born. From about age ten to fifteen, a boy goes through this second "birth" in both body and mind. In the movie *Spawn*, the hero struggled through death and rebirth because he didn't understand what was happening to him. In real life, for a lot of us, adolescence is like this. We don't understand what is happening to us.

Because I don't want you to have to go through your adolescence like that, I've written this book for you. If anything here doesn't make sense, I hope you'll ask your parents and other adults you trust to talk to you about it.

I spent my boyhood living in lots of different places, not only in different cities in the United States, but also in India and on a Native American reservation. I learned that boys everywhere want the same thing—to understand how to become men.

I think most things boys go through are normal. Every boy, as he's becoming an adolescent, and then a man, feels humiliated and weird, along with excited and proud. *Every* boy. No matter what any boy says, he feels the same emotions you do. *How* every boy gets through the years between ten and fourteen shows a lot about what kind of man he will become.

As you read this book about growing up, remember that if any word I use is unfamiliar to you, you can check your dictionary. One phrase I sometimes use is "a boy's clan." What I mean by that is all the people you trust—your parents, your grandparents, your friends, your parents' friends, your teachers, and coaches. You'll also notice some illustrations in this book. Your body now may not look like what these pictures show, but it will. The changes happen to everyone. So keep this book around for later. And enjoy becoming a man!

chapter 1

What's Happening To Your Body?

Sometime soon, if it hasn't started already, you're going to go through puberty. This is the time in your life when your body does more changing than it ever will again. Puberty generally starts between the ages of nine and fifteen and lasts from two to four years.

Nature's idea with puberty is to turn your little boy's body into an adult man's body.

Nature wants this to happen pretty quickly—not to take ten or twenty years. Why? Because for most people in other parts of the world (and for your own great-great-grandparents), having an adult's body by the middle teen years is very necessary. In most parts of the world, boys are working full-time by the age of fourteen; they have families of their own; they are fighting in wars.

But you live a life where you are not ready to have sex yet, or have a family of your own. You live a life where you don't have to work for a living; you don't have to fight in any wars at fourteen or fifteen. However, your body is the same sort of body that your great-great-grandfather had and that boys elsewhere in the world have. And so, by the time you're in your middle teens, your body, just like theirs, gets ready for sex, or work, or war.

In a way, your life is more difficult than your ancestors' lives. And in a way it's easier. It's easier because you can be a boy for a longer period of time than they could. You can spend your teenage years going to school rather than going to war or going to work full-time. It's harder because you get an adult's body before you know what to do with it.

A fourteen-year-old boy I knew at a school where I worked had this image of what it's like today for a boy to go through puberty. He said it's like you get a huge, interesting box of treasure before you know how to open it. It's a box *you* have to open, because the box is *you*. But there is no way you are able to understand it yet.

This description seems powerful to me. What boy isn't going to want to open the box? Every boy wants to. But you can't have sex yet because you don't know how or because you know you're just not ready. You can't go to work full-time at fourteen because you haven't learned enough in school to help you later in life. You have to go very slowly learning about this box, how to open it, and then how to use the powers that are inside.

Testosterone

There is a hormone inside your body called testosterone that controls a lot of what makes you a man. Hormones are chemicals that your brain releases. These hormones tell your body how to grow up. I'll talk a lot about testosterone throughout this book because it affects how your body changes, how you feel about sex, your moods and emotions, and your behavior.

Testosterone floods through your bloodstream during and after puberty. During puberty, you feel as if your body is emerging from a long winter. Think of testosterone as snow that has been falling in the mountains for a long time. A lot has accumulated up there. When puberty begins, the snow starts to melt and it floods all the streams and rivers in your body. This testosterone will flow really strongly through your body until you are about fifty or so. When you reach your late forties and early fifties—your dad's age or older—this flow of testosterone will ease up. By the time you are in your seventies or eighties—your grandfather's age—it will be a much smaller stream.

But puberty is the time of the strongest flood. You can get between five and seven surges of testosterone through your body every day. You'll probably bump into things a lot and think you're clumsy. Testosterone surges can cause that. You may also feel like masturbating a lot. We'll talk more about this in the chapter on sexuality. You may find yourself getting more ambitious about how successful you want to be in school or other parts of your life. You may find yourself getting into more fights (or at least getting more aggressive). You may find yourself liking more aggressive video games and movies. You may begin to think the only good hero is one who blows away all his enemies. You may want to be violent yourself, more than you know is right. You may egg on friends to do things that are risky—dangerous, illegal things, like driving a car before they've gotten a license, or immoral things, like stealing.

All these feelings can have a lot to do with the testosterone surges in your body. By the time you are sixteen or so, your body will have twenty times more testosterone than a sixteen-year-old girl has. Later we'll talk about ways in which girls and boys and women and men are just very different people. Testosterone is a big cause of those differences.

What Happens in Your Body During Puberty

During adolescence, you'll have a tremendous growth spurt. Testosterone surges trigger your growth spurt, which starts sometime between nine and fourteen. (If it hasn't begun by the time you're fifteen, you and your parents need to talk to a doctor.) You may grow taller than your mother or father by the time you are fourteen. Your arms will grow longer; your legs will grow larger. You may shoot up like a beanpole and think you'll be tall and skinny the rest of your life, but then your muscles will start to fill out and you'll be amazed at how strong you're getting to be.

You'll probably find yourself gaining weight before you grow much taller. You'll be eating a lot, growing out of clothes at the waist and at the seams. Then, just when you've gotten new pants to fit your bigger waist, they'll start becoming high-water pants because of your new tallness. All of this growth is normal.

Because of testosterone, most—but not all—of you will end up with bigger bones and more muscle than the young women you know. This won't happen to everybody. There are many men who are smaller than many women. Yet in most cases, if we measured their wrists (which is a good way to measure bone size), we'd probably find that even a six-foot-tall-woman won't have as large a wrist as a five-foot-tall man.

When you go through puberty, certain parts of you can get *really large,* and other parts of you may remain like a kid's. I remember one fourteen-year-old-boy who thought his nose was twice as big as the rest of his face. Well, in fact, he was in the middle of his growth spurt, and his nose was growing faster than other parts of his face. Of course, once he finished his growth spurt, things did even out and the rest of his face caught up to his nose. Unfortunately for this boy, it took a couple years. So don't be surprised if one part of you is bigger than another or out of proportion for quite a while.

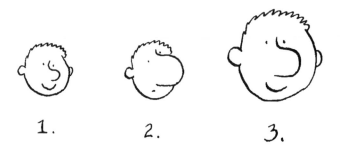

1.   2.   3.

I remember another boy who kept measuring his left arm and left foot. For almost a year, they were smaller than his right arm and right foot. No matter what I, or anyone else, told him, he was convinced he was an alien and would be like that for life.

During your growth spurt, your internal organs are also growing in size—your lungs, heart, brain. We'll talk more about the brain later. Organs like your heart and lungs grow much bigger and, as a result, give you the ability to run or dance for hours. During your growth spurt, if you're not involved in some kind of sport or martial arts or other physical activity, you ought to be. Karate, soccer, tennis—you name it. You need something to help train your lungs and heart so they work well for the rest of your life.

Body Hair, Voice Changes, Sexual Organs

Growing up means getting body hair, a much larger penis and testicles, and a deeper voice.

For about the first ten years of your life, you may have noticed a little hair on your arms and legs. It was pretty thin and very soft. Once puberty starts, more hair grows, and it gets a little coarser. It grows under your arms; where it didn't grow before. It grows on your face. It may grow on your chest and back, your buttocks, your knuckles. And, of course, at some point it will grow in a triangle just above your genitals, then maybe on your scrotum too.

I was talking to a class once, and a boy asked, "How come we get so much more hair than girls?" It's a good question. A lot of differences between boys and girls exist for this reason: For millions of years, our ancestors were what we call hunter-gatherers. The men hunted for food, and the women gathered roots and plants. The men were out in harsh weather, while the women spent more time in villages raising little kids. Because the men were out in the cold more, they needed more hair to keep their bodies warm. You have the same body as your long-ago male ancestors. You are growing hair in the same places they needed it to grow so they could stay warm.

Body hair is different for different ethnic groups, as you may have noticed in a locker room. Caucasian men tend to have more body hair than African-American men. We think the reason is that most Caucasian ancestors lived in cooler climates than most African ancestors. England or France is colder than Kenya or Zimbabwe. So white people needed more hair than black people. No one is absolutely sure if this is why, but it makes sense.

If you find yourself growing hair even in your ears, don't worry. Just think of your ancestors and why they needed it. If you don't find any hair growing on your chest, again, don't worry. However and wherever your hair grows, it will be about done growing by the time you are seventeen or eighteen. When you look at yourself naked in the mirror, you will see not only yourself but all your ancestors, too.

It's the same with your voice and your genitals. You are going to mature in these areas very much like those men in your family who came before you. Your voice may begin its change *before* you start growing more body hair. It usually takes about two years for your voice to change completely. Your voice may change before you start shaving. It will crack and go really high and then suddenly really low. It will probably do this at least once during a very embarrassing moment, like while you're in front of the class or trying to impress someone. You can either get really upset or just joke around and say, "Hey, there's an alien inside me!" or something like that.

Probably the most exciting and scary change your body goes through to become a man's body is the growth of your penis and testicles. When I was going through puberty, at first I thought I was crazy because I noticed my left testicle hanging down lower than my right. It is the normal way things happen, but I just didn't know. By the time puberty ends, your testicles and penis will have grown to be about eight times their size before puberty.

For every generation of boys, the size of the

penis and testicles can become kind of like an obsession. If you've stood at a urinal next to another boy and found your eyes wandering toward his penis, you're normal, even though it feels embarrassing to get caught. As you go

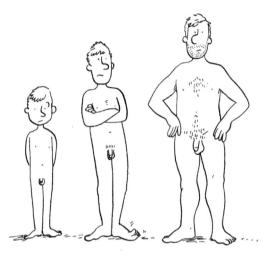

through puberty, you'll probably find all sorts of ways to compare your penis and testicles to other boys'. Your father and his father and his father and his father wondered about all the same things you're wondering about now.

Is mine big enough?

Is my friend's bigger?

Is there something wrong with me?

Why does it leak like that at night?

Why doesn't the hair on my scrotum grow more?

Can other guys see how small I am?

There are a thousand questions we ask during puberty, even if we never ask them aloud.

The facts about penis and testicle growth are a lot simpler than we might think.

Every boy's penis and testicles will grow in a way that the boy can feel okay about because there is no single right way for genitals to grow. There is no right size, no right amount of hair, no right "look." There's nothing we can do but wait and enjoy and accept ourselves.

Once a boy confessed to me that he thought if he masturbated a lot, his penis would grow bigger. He thought his penis was just too small and was afraid kids would tease him. He may have had fun masturbating, but masturbating does not help a penis grow. I suspect he didn't believe me when I told him this, and he probably went on masturbating to his heart's content!

While every penis is slightly different, especially when soft, the average grown man's fully

erect penis is around six inches, when measured from the pubus (where your triangle of
hair is). Guys will always joke about "eight
inches" or "mine drags on the floor when I
walk," but that's just talk and fun. Your penis
and all your friends' penises will be, by the
time you're sixteen or seventeen, about that
same six inches long.

No matter the size of your genitals (or the
size you think they are), size has nothing to do
with enjoyment or anything else. Even if
someone in the world had a ten-inch-long
erect penis (the world is full of variety, and
somewhere or another this man exists), he
would have nothing you don't have except a
little more weight to carry around!

Parts of puberty are embarrassing to go
through, but it is also an exciting time,
because it means you are becoming a man.
Anything that is important can be scary, and
that's what's behind the jokes and anxieties
about sex organs. Other people are scared,
and you are scared. It's that simple. And it's
okay. Every boy is scared when his body
begins the change to manhood. Not every

boy will admit it, and many men, even years later, will say, "Scared, no way, not me." But that's just b.s. We're all scared. It feels like there's an alien inside of us, and we feel *out of control.* There's no scarier feeling than that.

And the fact is that we really are not in control of the changes. Each of us is born with a genetic blueprint. Each boy's body is going to change the way his genes, his testosterone, and other parts of nature have determined it will change. We can't get our penises to be any bigger than they are going to be. We can't get our testicles to hang any lower than they are going to hang. We can't get more hair on our chests if nature doesn't make it grow there.

What we can control are these things:

• our behavior

• our attitudes toward others, like the people we love

• how much help we get in understanding what's happening to us

• how much patience we have

• how much courage we have to face the changes and the coming of manhood

- how honorable we are as we experiment with our new-found powers.

Other Fun Stuff

"You stink, man!"

"Hey, pizza face!"

"Don't touch me, you are drenched!"

Puberty brings with it fun stuff like body odor, acne, and lots of sweat. As testosterone moves through your bloodstream, it causes your oil and sweat glands to become more active. You are going to stink more than you ever have. You may want to use antiperspirants and cologne, but if you bathe frequently, you won't need to use these things as much. Some boys use antiperspirants and cologne because they think it's cool or they'll be more popular with girls. That's okay, but

 it's not necessary.

Acne can be a terrible problem for some boys. I had acne all the way into my twenties and then it stopped. I found out from my father that in our family, acne is pretty normal, just like getting gray hair in your twenties is normal on my mother's side. Acne, like body odor and genital size, is something to try to stay calm about. You can get dermatological aids to help with acne. Talk to your doctor or even your friends about what works and doesn't work. Also, you can joke about your acne and find ways just to take it in stride. There's no feeling worse than feeling ugly, so talk to your parents, friends, and other trusted adults. Don't bottle these feelings up.

Every boy sweats in his own way and in the quantity that his genetic blueprint has set up for him. Some boys are "sweaters," some aren't. Most boys will sweat more than most girls. A lot of this has to do with how testosterone affects male sweat glands. While sweating is generally not a big deal (if you bathe enough!), if you feel like you sweat more (or less) than others, talk to an adult you trust. Often you'll find that one of your parents, or your grandparents, or an uncle was a "sweater," and you have his genes.

What We Eat

What we eat *definitely* affects how much we sweat and also how we smell and how much acne we have. It can also affect our moods, emotions, feelings, and behavior. What we eat in adolescence is very important, but we tend to spend little time thinking about the foods we eat. We often eat what's in front of us or what the fad is. But what we eat is one of the things we can control, to a great extent, during adolescence.

Will it hurt you to eat a lot of burgers and fries?

Will it hurt you to eat more chocolate and sweets than you know you should?

Could you be allergic to certain foods and not know it?

The answer to these questions is often yes. As puberty begins and your body changes, talk to people who know about food and find out what is good and what is not good for you.

Check which foods you are allergic to. A food allergy can really affect how you use your brain and how you feel about life.

Make sure you're getting a lot of protein

(protein really helps your muscles grow) and the right amounts of fat and carbohydrates.

As much as possible, don't skip breakfast.

Avoid junk food. We eat junky stuff at parties, watching a football game, or at a movie, but boys who eat junk food daily are going to have problems during puberty—with body odor, acne, weight, and moodiness.

Drugs, Alcohol, and Cigarettes

During adolescence, we want to do things other people are doing, especially people we admire. We like to take risks just to show we can. We like to get a lift in life. Sometimes we don't like ourselves and just want to feel better.

And so we come to the question of cigarettes, drinking, and drugs. A cigarette one night under the bleachers at a ball game, or one beer here or there when you're fourteen or fifteen, is experimentation. Most boys experiment with something. Any adult who doesn't think so has forgotten what it's like to be an adolescent boy. However, if you are going through puberty and drinking, smoking, or taking drugs more than a little experimenting, you are in for trouble.

You will probably get sicker than others who are not drinking and doing drugs. Your brain cannot develop as well, so you won't be able to think and feel as much as you should be. Drinking leads to behavior you cannot control—like violence. You'll think you can be in control, but you can't. You'll find yourself in fights, or hurting your friends and family, and you'll wish you hadn't.

Cigarettes are the fastest thing you get addicted to. Cigarette companies *want* you to get addicted. They want you to be their customer for a long, long time. So they make advertisements just for you. Once you get addicted, you're more likely than other people to die at a young age, have health problems, stink of cigarettes, and just plain not be very attractive to a lot of the people you want to like you.

Remember that there is no way *not* to retard your maturing when you drink, smoke, or do drugs, especially during puberty and the growth years from ages ten to fifteen. Cigarettes, drugs, and alcohol are poisons to a body that is growing the way yours is. Each poison may cause only more acne, slower growth of your body and genitals, more anger, or bad moods. Or it may cause your early death. There is no way to avoid damage. The question is only, "When, in the next months or years, will I see just how much damage I have caused myself?"

Once your body becomes more adult, it doesn't absorb liquor or tobacco or drugs as quickly as your adolescent body. This is why adults and the law say you can't drink or smoke till you're a man. Sometimes you may feel as if adults don't trust you, or something like that, but in fact your body *can't* handle alcohol and tobacco. Even adults who drink or smoke too much or take drugs still die younger and get sicker and do meaner, crazier things than their friends who don't.

Sometimes kids will say, "Well, my dad did drugs in the sixties," or "My mom drinks." Talk to your parents about this. I think you'll discover that parents, if they took drugs or drank at a young age, probably did so after puberty. Most likely they experimented later in high school or in college, when their bodies and minds had done most of their developing. Almost all adults who did poison themselves during puberty—for instance, by smoking cigarettes habitually at twelve or thirteen—will tell you how much they regret it.

Just one last point: During puberty, there's so much you *can't* control—like how your hair will grow, when your genitals will grow, how your face will look. But drugs, alcohol, and cigarettes are things you can control by staying away from them.

When You Need Help with Puberty

I hope by now you have a clearer picture of what is going on or soon will start going on in your body. If you still have questions, go talk to your dad, mom, or another trusted adult. A lot of what's happening to you happened in much the same way to your father, uncles, and grandfathers, because you carry their genes. There is hardly anything you will experience that these men didn't experience, so don't be embarrassed about talking to them.

If none of these men is available to you, talking to any trusted male is going to help. That's because even without the "gene connection" of families, *all* men  went through changes like the ones you will be going through. No matter how strange, difficult, or unique what is happening to you may seem right now, *every* man has gone through something similar.

Here are some practical openers for getting a conversation started:

"I'm feeling _____. Is this normal?"

"Joe (or another friend) says _____. What do you think?"

"_____ happened today (or last week), and I felt _____. I'm confused and scared by these feelings. Can you help me?"

When I was almost fifteen, I hadn't gone through much of puberty yet. I remember constantly being embarrassed in the school locker room. Just about all the other boys my age were growing bigger and hairier and I wasn't. I thought there was something wrong with me. I wanted to die at times, I felt so humiliated.

I finally got the courage to talk to my father about it and found out that in my family there were lots of late bloomers—boys who went through puberty a little bit later than many other boys. This fact made me feel so much better. I saw that I was not the only person in the world who had felt this kind of embarrassment and humiliation. From talking to my dad, I also learned more about the men in my family, even ones who had died long before I was born. And, of course, I finally did mature into a man.

You are never alone as you're going through puberty. But if you don't work up the courage to talk to other men you trust, you will end up *feeling* alone.

chapter 2

What's Happening To Your Mind?

"What do you want from life right now?"

"I don't know."

"What do you need from life right now?"

"I don't know."

"What do you think is most important right now?"

"I don't know."

"What DO you know?"

(With a grin): "I don't know."

This is a real conversation I heard between a mother and twelve-year-old boy. Does it sound familiar? Even if you're not one of the "I don't know" boys or the "Uh huh" boys or the "I guess" boys, you know a lot of them. These are the boys who think about a thousand things but often won't share them with others, especially parents. These are the boys who just don't have the words to explain what's in their heads. We've all been these boys at some point, and we will be again.

During puberty, there is so much going on inside your mind, I can't possibly cover it in one chapter. And no one can know your mind, anyway. But lots of the thoughts and feelings that confuse you don't have to.

When you are around ten to fifteen, your mind goes through powerful changes—what psychologists call "the development of adult cognitive skills," or "the development of abstract intellect." To put it simply, just as your body is changing from a boy's to a man's, your mind is changing, too. Just as your penis, testicles, heart, lungs, muscles, and everything else is developing, so is your brain.

Boyhood is dying out in your brain, and man-hood is beginning. By the time these changes are complete, you will think about everything very differently.

Your Thinking Process, Including Your Sense of Values

Soon, if not already, you will be able to focus your attention for longer periods of time than you used to be able to do. You will like doing a hard crossword puzzle or a long science experi-ment all the way to the end, even if it takes hours. You will like studying something by looking at lots of alternatives.

You're able to see cause and effect better now, so grasping the deeper logic of moral issues becomes easier. Many times, you'll want to know *why* something is "wrong" when someone tells you it is. Though you won't say "Why, Mommy?" the way you did as a little boy, you're thinking about "whys" far more often. When you see a friend cheat on a test, you'll want to figure out in your head why it's wrong and how to handle the situation. You'll want to understand all the parts of the moral puzzle that cheating creates, and what your responsibilities may be.

You're discovering a whole new fantasy life. Don't be surprised if you fantasize about sex and violence. It's normal. If your parents and clan don't keep on showing you which acts of aggression are okay and which are not, you will make mistakes that hurt others. At the same time, you are getting old enough to figure out some of this dividing line for yourself without your parents' help. And you are definitely old enough to see that fantasizing about something is okay—it's just in your head and it's generally no one else's business—but that once you act on the fantasy, you're making it other peoples' business and often it won't be okay.

You will probably seek out one or two good friends to think things out with. Though you may ride bikes together or just play video games, you'll also reason with them and be challenged by them.

Your vocabulary will increase—with lots of new slang words and also lots of new technical words. You'll probably be swearing more now, too.

It's a confusing time when your brain is changing so greatly. On the one hand, you want to be sophisticated and mature. On the other hand, when you're around friends, being smart and sensible doesn't always feel as cool as using the word "shit." With this new brain of yours, you need to learn when to be cool and when to be more adult. To me, the most mature and admirable boy is the one who can be more adult with adults and have fun with his friends—including cursing and acting up in small ways some adults may not like. Even this acting up, though, is a challenge, because sometimes the boys will overdo the cursing and the dissing and you will have to stand up and tell them they're doing it. This is no easy balancing act.

Because of the changes in your brain, you're becoming more group-oriented in your thinking, so you're more susceptible to group-think. As much as you're developing your own intellectual powers, you're quite capable of giving in to someone who seems cooler. Even though you're getting smarter, you may often say, "I'm dumb; that guy's right. Joe gets it; I don't. I should think like Joe." Only *you* can decide whose thinking makes sense and whose doesn't. As always, trust your parents and clan to help with the big stuff. Never get so impressed with the way another person or group thinks that you give up your own take on things. Doing so is like letting your mind get stolen.

Let's Be Even More Specific About the Brain

There is a big difference in the way you think when you're ten years old and when you're thirteen. Boys at nine or ten years old have pretty concrete minds. The ten-year-old thinks about *this* TV show he is watching, *this* meal he's eating, right now. "The future" is pretty vague, except where it relates to something like going to the soccer game on Saturday.

The thirteen- or fourteen-year-old boy has a much more intellectual mind. He is beginning to puzzle everything out. *Everything!* At this age you can become like a lawyer. When I was fourteen, my parents called me "the fastest mouth in the West." I could and would debate *any* decision they made!

If you're a "legalistic, argumentative" boy like I was, you may drive other people nuts. You may drive yourself nuts, too! With your new abstract intellect, you figure everything in the world exists so that you can argue about it. Sometimes you'll think things out for so long, see so many sides of an issue, that you'll get exhausted or scare yourself or become very angry or sad. You may have trouble making decisions. You may become stuck by all the possibilities you now can see.

As all this is happening, it's important for you to remember that your brain may not change at the same time as your body. Your body may hit puberty early (let's say, at twelve), but your brain may not really start thinking abstractly till later.

Here are some good, clear signs that your mind is beginning to change in the way I'm talking about.

• You start to get jokes you never got before.

• You become idealistic. "The world ought to be…", "Why isn't it…" You create a picture in your mind of how some things should be, and get disappointed when the reality doesn't live up to your expectations.

• You become curious about new things, like driving a car before you're capable or taking something apart before you can put it back together again. Sometimes your curiosity gets you in trouble, and sometimes it leads you to make huge leaps in your understanding of how the world works.

• You discover the world of ideas and may suddenly devour lots of books.

• You discover a rich, sometimes frightening

fantasy life. It's probable that you fantasize not only about space ships and alien worlds, but also about sex. No doubt, many of the fantasies will seem bizarre to you, but that's quite normal. As your mind goes through its changes, it experiments with *everything.*

• You begin to think about the future—*your* future. Thinking about being an adult is exciting, but very scary, too. Again, this is where it's good to have a few relationships with adults and friends your age who are *really* trustworthy. You can talk to these people about adulthood and believe that what they tell you is meant to help you out.

These brain changes will continue at full speed during the middle-teen years and gain momentum and depth as you get to be fifteen and sixteen and seventeen. It's this way for all boys, even if they don't talk to one another about it a lot.

You and Your Anger

At this particular time of your life, you may get very angry. Not every boy does, but lots do. Parents can drive you nuts. You get rejected by people, and that makes you angry. Your hormones and the changes in your brain contribute to your anger. Often we get angry and feel good about it, but just as often we feel miserable after getting angry at Mom or Dad or a sibling or friend.

Here's a brief questionnaire for you to fill out. Also, if you want, your parents can fill it out—to get another opinion about yourself. I've adapted it from a quiz used by scientists at Harvard University. One of them especially, Dr. Ichiro Kawachi, has studied anger and its effects on health.

1. How many times a day do you feel like swearing out loud?
2. How many times a day do you actually swear out loud?
3. How many times a week do you feel like smashing something?
4. How many times a month do you actually break something?

5. How many times a month do you feel like picking a fistfight with someone?

6. How many times a year do you pick a fight with someone?

7. Do people call you "hot-headed" or "bad-tempered" or the like?

8. Do you often feel sorry afterward for being irritable and grouchy?

9. Do you often feel that you can't understand why you're this way or how to stop it?

10. How many times have you gotten so angry that you hurt someone physically?

If you *act* on your angry impulses frequently (for question 2, three times a day; for question 4, once a month; for question 6, once every six months); if you often feel guilty after an angry outburst and confused about its origins or how to control it; if you have a reputation among your family and friends as having a super-quick trigger; if you have hurt others in anger—these are all indications that you need help. You are in the first few years of adolescence, and these are the years in which to get the help. If you don't get the help now, your anger will only get worse.

Sometimes there will be people around you who truly don't understand you as you are now, the boy who is getting a man's body and man's brain. Perhaps they will not be able to see that although you are getting angry a fair amount, you're not *acting* on it, so it's not as big a problem as they think. Sometimes moms or teachers or dads or other people won't want you to feel angry. As much as you can, remind these people that there is a difference between feeling angry and acting out your anger. If you sulk and mutter and hit your punching bag or go into the garage and scream, you're being angry but not hurting other people with your anger. This kind of behavior is not only okay, it's often good for you. It gets the anger out of your body.

It's when you hurt other people that you have to worry. Anger is your own emotion and it is not meant to be used to hurt others. It is your responsibility to learn how to use and control it. If you are having trouble doing so, bring up the subject with Dad or a coach or some other man you trust, one who has learned how to use his anger. He can help you a lot. You might say, "Dad, I can't control my temper. What should I do?" Or, "Coach, I see you get angry at us, but you don't do it in a way that hurts us. Can you teach me how to do it like you do?" Or, "Grandpa, I don't understand why I get so angry so often. Can you help me?"

Boys learn to push down a lot of feelings like sadness or hurt and turn them into anger. Think of a boy at around eleven years old who smashes his knee on the corner of a table. He will probably curse or yell out in some way. His sister, of say, eleven or twelve, is more inclined to cry. Of course, some boys when they feel a terrible pain will cry tears and some will go completely silent. But I think you'll notice that lots more boys than girls will tend to yell and get mad at the table.

Boys and girls are different on the outside and on the inside. A boy's brain experiences, expresses, and releases the boy's feelings differently than a girl's brain does. When you're older, these differences will make more sense. You can also read other books I've written, like *Understanding Guys: A Guide for Teenage Girls*, which discusses the differences between adolescent male and female brains.

Not only are boys' brains a little different, but boys and girls also are taught to handle feelings differently. When a boy is upset, he often won't talk about it. Many of your friends may cope this way. You may, too. If you have a friend whose granddad has died, you may notice that rather than cry, your friend will clam up and look as if the least little thing will make him explode. In this example, the boy has turned his hurt into anger.

As much as you can, you need to *talk* about feelings when you're upset and even when you're happy. If all you can do is be angry, then *be* angry. Just don't hurt other people with your anger. You'll end up feeling worse...and even angrier—this time at yourself.

If you have an anger problem, one of the best ways to help yourself is to get into martial arts—they teach discipline, focus, maturity, and they're fun. Many churches, schools, and sports clubs also have "anger management" programs. You can try these, too.

A Rite of Passage

As your mind and body change, you want to know a lot more about what being a man is, and you want to be tested in ways that show you're becoming one. In a lot of countries, thirteen- or fourteen-year-old boys go through what is called a "rite of passage." It is a ceremony in which a boy's family and community teach him what a man is and show him how to leave childhood and enter adulthood. If you're Jewish or know Jews, you'll recognize this rite of passage in the *bar mitzvah*. At age

thirteen, after learn-
ing Hebrew pretty
well, a Jewish boy
stands up in front of
the whole congrega-
tion and shows every-
body what he knows.
The rabbi and the
boy's parents and all the people call him a
man and invite him to join the Jewish community as a man.

Whether you realize it or not, your mind
searches for people who can help you
through a rite of passage. You also look for
experiences—tests—that you see as a rite of
passage. This is part of what you're doing
when you experiment with cigarettes, or jump
off a high cliff into a lake even though you're
scared, or tell your mom or dad to bug off.
You're trying to teach yourself what being a
man is, even though if you choose something
like smoking, you're choosing a dangerous
life-threatening rite. Every boy wants a rite of
passage and needs one to grow up. A lot of
families don't have them because they've for-

gotten that boys need them. So you may have to remind your family, your church, and your adult friends about this need.

Find something that fits *your* life and who *you* are. You will have fun, you will understand how meaningful life is, and you will feel like a man. There is nothing better than having the people you love see that you are becoming a man, for real.

chapter 3

Let's Talk About
Sex and Love

One of my favorite things to do at school parents' nights or at conferences where I've been asked to speak is to ask the men to confess how many times a day they used to masturbate or wanted to masturbate when they were around fourteen. Generally, the average is one to two times a day. There is usually at least one man who laughs and says, "Once a day? Try five times a day." And of course there are some men who recall masturbating once a week, or even (though rarely) not at all.

Masturbation is just one of the ways a boy feels sexual. Masturbation is very natural. It's a far better thing to do at your age than to have sex with a girl. You're not ready for sex with a girl, but you're ready for your penis to get erect, and you're ready to rub it until you ejaculate—when semen spurts from your penis. It feels good; it releases tension; and there's nothing wrong with it. Most boys masturbate when it's appropriate and know the truth about the boys who *say* they're having sex, but in fact are doing exactly what you're doing: masturbating.

Something else nearly every boy experiences is wet dreams. You wake up in the morning with the sheets sticky and wet under you. These sticky spots come from semen that leaks out of your penis during the night.

Something else that happens to nearly all boys is getting erections at the *weirdest* times, sometimes in the middle of class because the sun came in the window on your groin, or even just because your pants rubbed against your penis in a certain way. Often you get an erection during one of your testosterone surges. Remember, in puberty, you can get between five to seven surges of testosterone through your blood every day. A surge can happen late in the night and cause the erection and wet dream while you sleep. Other surges happen during the day, for instance, during a science experiment in afternoon lab. Your body needs to have these erections and wet dreams so it can do its sexual growing up, so don't worry about them. They're normal.

How Sex Actually Works

You've probably learned about sexual intercourse from your parents and clan, and heard the information again in sex ed. class at school, but it can't hurt to go over the basics once more.

The sex act between a man and a woman generally starts out with the sharing of nice words and feelings, then maybe some kissing and hugging and stroking. This is what's called foreplay. During foreplay, a man and woman get more and more sexually aroused. When actual intercourse occurs, the man's erect penis enters the woman's vagina. The friction between the tender inside of the vagina and the tender skin of the erect penis can make both the man and the woman "come"— reach a climax. Men and women climax in different ways, of course. The woman, usually because her clitoris is stimulated enough, will have an orgasm that will make her body shudder and make her feel good. It doesn't show up in the obvious way of the man's orgasm— ejaculation.

The man's come, or semen, is a milky river

of little sperm. These sperm are like tiny fish. They squiggle up through the woman's cervix, a narrow opening near the end of the vagina, and keep swimming toward the uterus, which is about the size of a small fruit. The uterus is what, during pregnancy, expands to carry the baby. The sperm swim through the uterus toward two tubes, called the fallopian tubes. These tubes connect the uterus to the ovaries. The ovaries make the eggs that the sperm are looking for. Once a month, an egg drops down into one of the fallopian tubes, and that's generally where the sperm find it.

Once the sperm find an egg, the many little sperm hit it over and over and over again. Remember, there are millions of sperm in every male ejaculation. Thousands die while they're hitting the egg, but maybe one lives. If this one lives and gets into the egg, fertilization occurs. The woman becomes pregnant.

Sometimes boys will say, "Well, a girl can only get pregnant at a certain time of the month, right in between her periods. We just won't have sex around that time so she can't get pregnant." Wrong! There are cases all over the world, including in your own town, of girls getting pregnant at supposedly safe times. Girls themselves have thought they were safe, but have gotten pregnant. There is really no way you can know from the outside what is really happening inside a girl.

The plain fact is that young teenage boys are physically able to make babies, but they are not emotionally ready to become fathers.

Sex Is Always About Choosing

There are some basic things I think you absolutely have to know in order to make good choices about sex—and that goes for everything from masturbation, which you may be doing already, to sexual intercourse which you will have when you get a lot older. This advice will help you make good choices about not only what you *do,* but also how to *feel* about what you do. Some of this advice won't apply to you because you aren't thinking about these things yet. But keep this book around. One day you will be thinking about this stuff a lot.

Sexual intercourse is a very important part of life and something you don't want to do just for the hell of it. You have to respect it like you respect other things in life that are sacred and special. It is something a man and woman share after they have known each other a very long time and have grown to love each other in a way they'll never love anyone else. When we say we "love" somebody, we don't mean we just have a crush or just fantasize about a girl. We mean we've developed a closeness with her in which we can talk about nearly anything together, and we want to spend many, many years in the closest possible relationship.

If people in your clan say not to have sexual intercourse till you're married, listen to them and find out why they say this. At least wait until you're in your late teens and until you've come to care about and love a girl or woman for longer than the "time of hormones." The time of hormones is when you feel like you just want to have sexual intercourse because your body is surging with testosterone. (A girl's body is also surging with hormones—the female ones—estrogen and proges-terone.) Male hormones drive boys toward having orgasms. But boys are not men yet—they're not yet capable of having the kind of emotional relationships with women that I just described. And they're not yet ready to treat sexual intercourse as one of life's most special and sacred things.

When a man and a woman do have sexual intercourse, they must *always* practice safe sex, which generally means using a condom. Remember that if a man puts his erect penis into a woman's vagina, he can make her preg-nant at any time that it's in there. It doesn't matter whether he comes or not. A penis can leak semen at various times when it's erect and even before it's completely erect. Except for when a man has an orgasm and ejaculates, he won't notice most of these leakages. And this semen creeps into the woman even if a man "pulls out"—so she can get pregnant without a man coming.

Although puberty is not the right time to have sexual intercourse, there are a lot of things boys and girls can do to have some sexual intimacy with each other. They can masturbate each other, for instance. These sorts of things can help the boy ejaculate and help the girl reach an orgasm. Then the need for actual sex in his body eases up for a time. Doing these things is more appropriate than having sexual intercourse. So staying a virgin till you're married or until you're older and very much in love doesn't mean you and a girl won't be able to do sexual things together. It does mean you won't put your penis in a girl's vagina.

When you feel ready, you ought to talk to the adults you trust most about when they first had sex and what it was like. Don't just go off alone in your room or with other boys your age to think about it. I didn't have sexual intercourse till I was twenty and in college. I did other experimental things in high school, but never the actual act of putting my penis in my girlfriend's vagina. I made a good choice to wait till I was old enough to understand what I was doing. If you talk to adults about sex, they'll tell you stories like mine, and you'll be able to make sensible choices.

Testosterone is a sex hormone, so your body will want to ejaculate *a lot* once you reach puberty and as you go through adolescence (and, in fact, on into adulthood). Don't be surprised if you want to ejaculate more than once a day. Remember, it's natural to feel this way, and it's natural to ejaculate in ways that don't involve intercourse.

At age eleven or twelve, you may begin experimenting with *both* boys and girls. Sometimes boys are surprised to learn that experimenting with other boys is normal. One boy I know was crying one day, and I couldn't get him to talk about why. Finally, he decided to trust me and he said he was crying because he and another boy had been masturbating in front of each other and he felt ashamed. Even more than that, he thought now he was homosexual. I helped him see that what he was doing was normal. I also talked to him about homosexuality—what it is and what it isn't.

Sometimes boys think if they experiment sexually with other boys, they're homosexual. It's not true. As I just said, sexual experimentation with other boys is normal. "Circle jerks," where boys sit around masturbating and see who comes first, happen a lot. Sometimes a boy and a friend touch each other, even masturbate each other. It is normal experimentation and a learning time for boys.

New scientific evidence shows us that people are born homosexuals or heterosexual. For homosexual boys, there is probably a little piece of the hypothalamus (this is a part of the brain) that is different from a heterosexual boy's. This difference may account for homosexuality.

Some people hate others who are homosexuals. If you feel this way, you should take a close look at yourself. Are you scared that if you don't hate a gay person, people may think you are gay? Are you frightened that you may be approached in a sexual way by someone who is gay? You don't need to hate homosexual people, and if you're not homosexual, you don't have to think you are. If you see someone saying hateful things, or being mean to a gay person, do anything you can to help the boy who is getting hurt *and* help the boy who is doing the hating to see that his hate is wrong. As you struggle with these situations, talk about your worries and fears with a trusted adult who can give you reassurances as well as good advice.

If you are homosexual, you will have had powerful feelings of sexual attraction to other boys and men probably since you were young, or since the beginning of puberty. You will not want just to experiment with other boys; you'll want to really, really like, and eventually fall in love with, other boys.

Although I am not going to discuss homosexuality extensively here, there are many books for teenagers on the subject. If you think you might be gay, or if you are just plain curious about homosexuality, you may want to read more. *Two Teenagers in Twenty: Writings by Gay and Lesbian Youth,* edited by Ann Heron (Alyson Publications, Inc., Boston, 1994) and *Changing Bodies, Changing Lives: A Book for Teens on Sex and Relationships,* by Ruth Bell (Vintage Books, New York, 1987) are two books that I would recommend. You can go to the library to find other titles, or if you would like to speak with someone directly, you can contact youth and/or gay advocacy organizations in your area. You can find their phone numbers in the yellow pages.

Boys and girls often think about sex differently. Because of testosterone, because of your male brain, and also because of the way your culture and family raise you, you think about sex one way, just as there are biological and cultural reasons why a girl thinks about sex in another way. These differences between boys and girls—how they think about sex, what it means to them, how they fantasize about it, how they think it fits in their lives,

how often they want it, when they want it, why
they want it—don't show up all the time. But
they do crop up often enough to cause a lot of
confusion and hurt. At your age, the best
thing to do is talk to adults you trust so that
when you get older and start having sex, you'll
understand the different needs men and
women have.

What you will really want from another person, like a serious girlfriend, is love and emotional support, not just sex. But teenage boys
often don't realize that and so sometimes pur-
sue sex and miss the love. Part of becoming a
man is having sexual intercourse with a part-
ner when you are emotionally ready. But it's
only a small part. The biggest part of becoming a man is learning how to be close to a person—learning to talk with her, listen to her,
wonder about her, tell her the story of your
life, and learn who she is. In a few years, some
of your friends may become obsessed with getting laid. But you can grow up better by masturbating or doing other things to fulfill your
sexual urges, and spending as much time as
possible now listening to and talking to peo-

ple you trust about what you feel and what you think.

Television commercials and a lot of television shows are trying to get you to have sex before you are ready. They're doing this because they think you're stupid enough to buy whatever they want you to buy if you are convinced that their particular product will help you have sex. It's hard right now for your clan to protect you from these shows and commercials, so you have to protect yourself.

You have to talk back to the television. When you see a commercial trying to manipulate you, diss the commercial out loud or in your head. For instance, when you see a used-car dealer trying to sell a car by having a woman with big breasts in a bathing suit lie on the hood, find out the name of the dealer and do everything you can to make sure no one you know buys a car there. The owners hope we're all stupid enough to think the sexy girl will be ours if we buy the car.

There is no way at your age *not* to be confused and a little crazy about sex. There is nothing you can do but be patient (one day, in about twenty years, it will make sense) and talk to adults you trust.

Falling In and Out of Love

There's also no way not to be a little crazy about love. It's just part of life.

Just as much as your body and mind are changing, your "heart"—your ability to love people—is changing, too. For a few years you'll be a little interested in girls but not too interested. But by the time puberty is over, you'll be very interested. (If you are homo-sexual, substitute the word "boys" for "girls.")

There's no one right way to fall in love, and there's no right time. Some boys don't really like someone seriously until they're seventeen or even twenty. Some ten-year-old boys want girlfriends.

There's no way to avoid being hurt as you go through the process of learning what love is. You will fall in love and be reject- ed a number of times. You will say things you regret and your girlfriends will say things they regret. You will get so mad you can't see straight and so sad you think you are going to die.

As with everything else in this adventure of adolescence, it is important for you to turn to parents and clan to help you make your way. Here are some things to think about as this "love stuff" starts happening to you over the next few years.

Boys and girls are afraid of each other, even though they rarely admit it. Boys tremble and shake just thinking about calling girls they

like.   (Girls do the same with boys.)   It's
scary—and thrilling.

Already, if you see a girl you like standing in
the hall at school, your body can become
tingly with excitement.   But chances are you
don't go up and talk to her because you are

afraid.   You're afraid
you'll do something
foolish. (And you *will* do
many foolish things in
the next few
years!)   You're
afraid she'll just
turn away and
walk on as if you didn't exist.   If you aren't old
enough yet to have gone through these situations, you will, and you have probably noticed
them happening to an older brother or sister
or someone else who is learning about love.

It's normal to be scared of girls.   Often you
can't talk to other boys, even your good
friends, because boys your own age aren't
mature enough to admit they are afraid, too.
They would rather wear their armor all the
time and say, "You wuss, I'm not scared."

What's the best thing you can do? Talk to adults about your fears. They will help you. They have felt the same fears. I can tell you that the fears  will never go away completely, not even when you are an old man. They are a normal part of life. Men and women are afraid of each other, too. That fear ends up being, by the time you are an adult, something you learn not to be afraid of. That may sound like a contradiction, but it's true.

Often it feels like girls know a lot more about emotional things than boys. Often they do. A girl may pretend to know very little (so a boy she likes can feel like he's the smartest thing around!) but really she may know a lot more than the boy about relationships, romance, sexual attraction and adult life. Why? Because girls often mature faster and earlier than boys.

In general, girls begin puberty a year or two earlier than boys. And while it usually takes boys about four years to finish puberty, it takes girls only around three years. You may be thirteen and not have started puberty yet, but a girl at thirteen may be almost done. So girls often are thinking and learning about love before boys are.

Also, as I mentioned before, there are differences between the ways girls' brains work and boys' brains work. These differences make most girls better at talking about love and other feelings. In this area, most boys are at a disadvantage.

So it's very important for you as a boy to realize that a lot of girls who are your age are more mature right now. But don't worry. By the time you are an adult, you'll have caught up!

At your age, there are more important things than really liking a girl. School, your community life, your family life, your friendships, your time with your grandparents, time out in nature, playing sports—these are far more important right now than trying to push yourself to have a girlfriend. Sometimes a boy will think—maybe after he has watched adults or a romantic movie—that if he can just get a girlfriend, he'll know everything there is to know, he'll be a man, he'll feel great about himself.

It's not true. Just like having sexual intercourse doesn't make you a man, getting a girlfriend doesn't either. Becoming a man is a much more complicated journey through all sorts of feelings, relationships, and experiences, which we'll explore more carefully in the next chapter.

chapter 4

What's Happening with Your Relationships?

Puberty is a trial-and-error experience, not just in the way you try out your new body, with its surging hormones, but also in the way you try out your new mind, with its abstract thinking powers. It's not just in the way you feel sexually and romantically, but in so many other feelings and emotions too that deeply affect your relationships. If you were once a "sweet little boy," don't be surprised if now you become more aggressive with people. Or if you used to be a "tough little boy," you may now become quieter, more sensitive with people. Puberty allows you to experiment with new selves and relationships.

Here are some things you may go through between the ages of ten and fourteen, things you might not notice unless someone points them out. Once you know what they are, you can be ready for them and can use your knowledge of them to help you in your relationships.

You can see your maleness better now and how it's different from femaleness. To become the sort of man you want to be, talk in more depth with your parents and teachers and grandparents about what they think a man is. Ask them things like, "What do you think is the most important thing about being a man?" Or, "What does it mean to be an honorable, responsible man?" Or, "When did you know you were a man?"

You may really want to hang out with a group of guys, but you'll also feel like doing everything yourself. It is very confusing. You'll resolve your conflict sometimes by pulling away from parents toward your friends; sometimes by pulling away from friends toward parents; and sometimes by pulling away from everyone just to be by yourself. With each tug and pull, you'll be trying to find out who you are. It is helpful to keep a journal, handwritten or on a computer, so you can write about and think through confusing times.

As you move through puberty, you will probably become either more boisterous or more subdued, more happy at times or more worried at times. Perhaps around friends you'll act up more, but around your family you'll be a silent lump. Much of this behavior is normal.

You'll become self-conscious about your skills, your appearance, and your behavior— lots of things, and at times just about everything. These feelings also are normal. It helps for you to be aware when you're becoming anxious and not to take it too seriously. You'll work hard, do the best you can, and the cold sweats and nervousness will pass.

You'll probably become more sensitive than before about being criticized, and you might even become a little paranoid about ridicule. Much of this you may, if you're a quiet type of guy, keep to yourself. The more you can talk with people you trust, the better you'll feel.

You're going to be also more critical of yourself than before, but you may hide that by criticizing others. With eleven- and twelve-year-old boys I like to say, "You're dissing Joe, but a lot of the things you're making fun of are things you really don't like about yourself." Confronting what you don't like in yourself can't hurt—not much, at least.

While you may be talking to your parents less than before and telling them less about your feelings, you are also developing new abilities to care for others. You're seeing more of how people can feel hurt and how to help. This quality developing in you is wonderful, so don't hide from it. Let yourself care.

Don't be surprised if you want to be alone a lot, reading, watching television, listening to music. You need this time alone. You will be soaking up new ideas like a sponge. You will be watching Michael Jordan, John Elway, Andre Agassi, and a hundred other role models on TV. You will be reading about strange, faraway worlds and wondering if you can ever go there.

 In all the hundreds of ways you spend your time with new images and ideas, you will be finding tiny

pieces of yourself and putting them together. Most of the time you will not even notice yourself doing this. Just make sure to judge whether the images you are soaking in are good for you. If someone you trust tells you they're not, honor that person's judgment for now. He or she is probably right.

You'll seek out opportunities to make your own decisions, and you'll show, in small ways, that your parents no longer have control over how you react to things. You still need to obey your parents. But at the same time, you'll find yourself in places where your parents aren't, so you'll have to make a lot of decisions on your own.

You'll probably do things your parents tell you not to do. I remember my parents forbidding me to go to a certain movie. Of course, I sneaked in with my best friend, Stan. My parents found out, and I got in trouble. But this is the kind of thing boys your age will do. Problems come in when you break the really big rules, the important ones, the ones you know will affect whether your parents continue to trust you. You never want to break these big rules, because once trust is broken, sometimes you can't repair the hurt, no matter how much you want to.

You'll appear not to need parents and family. But you still need the emotional safety net of parents and family as much as ever. You just don't tend to show it to them often, or as clearly. That's okay. It's also okay and right to show it at the very important times. No one will ever love you the way your family does.

You and Your Mother

You'll find yourself starting to pull away from your mom. At some point between the time you're ten and fourteen something will happen in you that seems to say, "I love Mom, but she doesn't understand me so I just don't want her talking to me, telling me what to do, or touching me as much." That feeling is both scary and normal. As a boy begins his journey to manhood, he realizes, even if he never says it aloud, that his mother is not a man and can't understand certain things about being a man.

Once I was in a grocery store and watched a

thirteen-year-old boy using the F word at his mother, calling her a bitch and telling her she was shit. He was pulling away from his mother by abusing her. This is the wrong way to do it.

It's better to remain respectful of your mother even though you may share fewer secrets with her and do more things without her now. Also remember, your mother may not have the easiest time with your adolescence. Often moms can try to hold a kid back without even realizing it. If you think your mother isn't letting you go, try to tell her how you're feeling—always with love and respect.

"Mom, I don't want to hug you right now, but I love you."

"Mom, I feel bad right now. I just need to be by myself for a while."

The biggest thing that happens when you start to separate from your mom and become an independent adolescent is that you take control over your own feelings. At the same time, there's often no one like your mom to talk to. She understands so much about girls, about you, about life. So make an effort to

explain how you'd like things to be now.

"Mom, I'm starting to feel differently toward you, but I love you and still want to talk to you. Can we do it this way for a while?" Then fill her in on what you want. It won't always work the way you'd like, but at least you and she will be able to talk about this confusing time between mothers and sons.

You and Your Father

As you reach the ages of ten and eleven and then go into puberty, you need your father and other men a lot more. They know what being a man is, and you need to learn about that from them. You need to ask questions about all the changes you are going through. You need to spend time with them, even if you're just silent together. You need to watch them work and talk and cry and laugh. For a boy your age, there is nothing quite like a father or other father-like man who takes an interest in you, looks you in the eye, and says, even if he never uses words, that you are important, you are smart, you are becoming a man.

If you don't like your father, this is a time to try to get help in figuring out why. Most fathers are great guys even though sometimes they drive us nuts. And they do know more than you do right now about being a man.

If your father isn't around because your parents are divorced or separated, don't give up

on him until you have no other choice. Try to learn from him what you can. If your mother is really mad at him and trying to keep him away from you, tell her that you need your father and you don't want to hear any more about how much she hates him.

If your father is dead, lives far away, or just refuses to see you, make sure to become friends with one or more other good men— like your grandfathers, uncles, a teacher, a coach, a friend's father, a Big Brother, or a Boy Scout father—so that you can learn what a man is and be admired by these men for the special person that you are.

I remember one boy whose father was a workaholic. The boy turned twelve, and once again, his father was away on business for his birthday. The boy got up the courage to tell his father how mad and disappointed he was. And it didn't take just one conversation. It took a number of times before, finally, his father understood how much his son needed him. The father did start to work a little less and be around a little more.

Often, fathers have to work so hard that they just get used to not being home a lot and not being available to their kids. These fathers forget that when their sons are nine, ten, or eleven, and as they move into puberty, they *really* need fathers or other men like fathers to help them. So it may be up to you to remind your father of how important he is to you now!

School Life

During puberty, how you act in school can change a lot. You'll probably have a little more difficulty handling failure now—especially in certain academic or athletic areas you care most about—than when you were seven or eight. This is very normal.

You'll probably become more competitive because how you compare to your friends takes on new importance. You may not be competitive in all areas—for instance, you may not care much about sports—but you may be competitive about getting good grades or being in a band or a club. It's good to be more competitive because it means you're challenging yourself and your friends to do better. If you get *too* competitive—where you think that you always have to be the best—you need to remind yourself that you can play a game or take part in an activity just for the fun of it.

You'll probably debate more with teachers and authority figures. You'll want to think for yourself. It's important to pick and choose what you are going to argue about. Some boys like to argue about *everything*. They don't get very far and start losing friends as well as the respect of the teachers and others who really do care about them.

The transfer from elementary to junior high school can be very hard. There's no getting around that. If you are a boy who has already started to mature physically, you may find the adjustment easier. Smaller, less mature boys may look up to you. Girls may, too. And if you're starting junior high with some of your best friends, that makes the switch easier, too. But if you're a late maturer or you have no friends—maybe you just moved to a new city—it can be one of the most difficult experiences of your life. I once worked with a boy who got beat up four times in the first month of junior high. He was a late maturer, and he had a big temper. He picked fights and dissed other people a lot. He thought he could make up for being a late bloomer by showing other people how tough he was. It didn't work. He just ended up feeling bad. The best thing you can do during the hard days and months is be patient (you will adjust in time), try to make new friends, and rely on people you love and trust.

Friends

As you begin puberty, more and more of the information you get will come from friends—information about sex, cigarettes, alcohol, drugs, and so on. You'll try to be like your friends in more ways than before, wanting the same shoes, the same video game, maybe the same nose ring. There's nothing wrong with trying to be like your friends, but there's something wrong with trying to change who you are just so you will be liked.

Life is very hard if you can't depend on friends for a sense of belonging. If you have no friends, or if everyone your age makes fun of you and pushes you out of games, activities, and conversations, you will feel miserable. Most kids go through this situation. When you have these bad times with kids your own age, remember to rely on your family and maybe one best friend. It always does end, so that's a good thing to remember (though it may not help when you're feeling alone and like an outcast).

It's natural to want to be important among your group of friends. You'll probably feel some confusion; the urge to be in one clique, then another; the sense of never quite knowing where you belong; the pull to do what parents say, but also what friends say. There's no way to avoid the confusion. It just goes along with this stage of your life. As always, trust your parents and other adults to help you understand what you're going through and how to make the best decisions.

closing words

I hope that this book has helped you learn more about yourself. When I was writing this book, I talked a lot to my editor, Jane O'Connor, about what it was like to be your age. I said to her: "You know, when I was ten, eleven, twelve, and around that age, adults didn't talk with me enough about meaningful things. When they did, they didn't go into enough detail, maybe because they thought I was too young to get it. And what they left out was often really important. I would have been able to get it. All they had to do was tell me what I needed to know."

Jane said, "Yeah, it wasn't any easier for me as a girl. I was clueless. No kid who is becoming an adolescent wants to be clueless."

Well, in this book I hope I have given you details—good, interesting, juicy details—so you are not clueless. If you think I've left something out or if you have questions, write me at the address that's at the back of this book. I hope as you become a man you'll refer back to certain sections, pass the book on to friends or younger brothers, and talk about different points with friends and the people you trust.

There's an old story you probably know about a boy named Jack who sets out one day with an old cow on a tether. The cow is no longer giving milk and must be sold so the family can have some money to buy food. Jack meets a man who says, "Hey, where are you going with that cow? I've got some magic beans if you'll trade me the cow for the beans." Jack feels adventurous and wants to have some magic in his life, so he agrees to the trade.

"Jack and the Beanstalk" is a story you probably read when you were a little boy. Did you know that it's actually a story about a boy your age—somewhere between ten and fourteen—who sets out on the path to manhood? The magic beans turn into a beanstalk, which Jack climbs. He reaches a giant's castle, where he discovers a goose that lays golden eggs, a magic harp, a lot of treasure, and a maiden. Jack grows up during this adventure. When the giant tries to get him, Jack runs back down the beanstalk, then cuts it down so the giant falls and dies.

You are a lot like Jack, discovering magical things about yourself, digging into your treasure box, learning who you are, facing your deepest fears (the giant), finding romance (the maiden), discovering important talents in yourself (the goose that laid golden eggs), and listening to beautiful sounds and voices, like the magic harp's, which will keep guiding you on your journey of self-discovery.

In this book, I've been the man with the magic beans. I hope you'll plant these beans well, study them, think about them, follow them up the beanstalk and toward your man-

hood. I hope you'll get help from all the people you need along the way. The next few
years of your life are going to be exciting and
confusing. A little magic never hurts!

Michael Gurian
P.O. Box 8714
Spokane, WA 99203
www.michael-gurian.com

A BOOK FOR THE
PARENTS AND TEACHERS
OF ADOLESCENT BOYS

Michael Gurian's
A Fine Young Man

A *New York Times*
Bestseller

"This book is filled with stories and practical advice for parents and
teachers of adolescent boys. Michael Gurian takes a thoughtful look
at nature and nurture, and at the role of culture and testosterone in
the lives of boys. I recommend it to all who want to raise fine young
men."

—Mary Pipher, author of *Reviving Ophelia*

"*A Fine Young Man* convincingly illustrates. . . the peculiar pain and
potential loneiness of being a boy in America today."

—*Time*

"Proactive and ultimately imbued with hope. With persuasive
eloquence, Gurian outlines thoughtful and practical steps"

—*Publishers Weekly* (starred review)

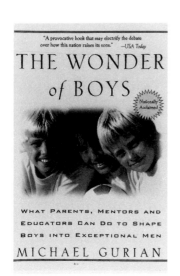

ALSO BY MICHAEL GURIAN

*The Wonder of Boys: What
Parents, Mentors and Educators
Can Do to Shape Boys into
Exceptional Men*

THE NATIONAL BESTSELLER

"*The Wonder of Boys* became the impetus for a growing 'boys move-
ment'. . ."

—*USA Today*

"Full of good insights and advice."
—*Los Angeles Times*

"*The Wonder of Boys* will help future generations open the lines of
communication between men and women by giving us what we need
to raise strong, responsible, and sensitive men."

—John Gray, author of *Men Are from Mars,
Women Are from Venus*